AF478313

The Marblehead town seal, p. 9, and the painting of "The Spirit of '76," p. 16, are reproduced by permission of the town Board of Selectmen. The original painting hangs in the Selectmen's Meeting Room in Abbot Hall, Marblehead, Mass.

The 1918 masthead of the *Marblehead Messenger*, pp. 40-41, is reproduced by permission of the *Marblehead Reporter* (Lynn Sears, Editor).

Printed in the United States of America
First printed March 1993

Hardscratch Press, Walnut Creek, California

Library of Congress Catalog Card Number: 92-75702

ISBN: 0-9625429-5-4

1 2 3 4 5 6 7 8 9 0

POST CARD

QUALITY

MESSAGE MAY BE WRITTEN ON THIS SIDE.

ADDRESS ONLY ON THIS SIDE.

U.S. POSTAGE
ONE CENT

PUBLISHED BY LEONARD P. THORNER. MARBLEHEAD, MASS.   MADE IN GERMANY.   29382

These where were
very good, many but
I couldn't taste
the vinegar at all.
M.P.C.

Mrs. Harold K. Lord,
Sanford,
Me.

Box # 733

Z 1180 HARBOR VIEW FROM ABBOT HALL TOWER; MARBLEHEAD, MASS
PUBLISHED BY LOUIS A. RADELL, MARBLEHEAD, MASS.
COPYRIGHT 1912 F. B. LITCHMAN

MCML

Mary Cole Mason Lord, 1887-1988

Stories collected by Martha Mason Lord Getchell

A Hardscratch Press Book

A FORTUITOUS SERIES OF people and circumstances came together to form this book:

An exceptional woman born and brought up in Marblehead, Massachusetts, who had complete recall of events until her death at age 101. (She also had a wonderful insistence on dating every photo she collected and identifying everyone pictured.)

Her photographer brother-in-law, my Uncle Fred Litchman, who had a flair for capturing occasions and in whose house my sister, Elizabeth, and I spent summer vacations. Elizabeth has encouraged me and read parts of the book as it has proceeded and loves it.

MCML's granddaughter, Deborah Lord Boelter (daughter of my late brother, Robert Lord), who lives in Homer, Alaska, and has cheerfully lent her skill typing and retyping my manuscripts. She and her sister, Leslie Lord Roth of Kenai, Alaska, and brother, Terry Lord of Fairbanks, as well as Elizabeth's son, Michael Armitage, all have kept an interested eye on my progress.

The readiness of my husband, Nelson, to sustain me in this project.

Reacquaintance with an old friend, Jackie Pels, who came to Washington, D.C., from Alaska as a girl seeking a job and landed one in Nelson's office. She and her Hardscratch Press partner, David Johnson, have turned my collection of MCML's stories into a book Mother would have approved of.

Martha Mason Lord Getchell
Seneca, South Carolina
December 14, 1992

The Lord family: Mary (MCML), Martha, Robert, Harold and Elizabeth,
with cousin Edith Mason Bowden (far right), Aug. 28, 1922.

Introduction

Mary cole mason lord (mcml) was born at Marblehead, Massachusetts, on March 26, 1887, and died at Leesburg, Virginia, June 15, 1988, three months into her 102nd year.

MCML had three children: myself, Martha Mason Lord Getchell, 76 as I write this; my sister, Elizabeth Ellen Lord Armitage, three years older, who lives in Florida and Hampton Beach, New Hampshire; and our brother, Robert Wentworth Lord, deceased in the summer of 1990, who was six years younger than I and lived in Homer, Alaska.

Mother lived in Emery Mills, Maine, after our father died in 1945. At age 58, she learned to drive, and she designed and was the contractor of her house beside the stream that runs out of Mousam Lake. She worked for several years at the York Utilities Co. office between Sanford and Springvale, Maine. Her next and last job was as admitting officer at the Sanford Henrietta D. Goodall Hospital, where she was a knowledgeable and responsible member of the staff. She was on hand to process the birth certificates for two of her grandchildren, Robert's daughters, Deborah (1948) and Leslie (1955). She retired in the mid-1960s.

After she retired, she traveled. She visited Elizabeth and her husband, Pete, who lived in Annapolis, Maryland, and then me, while my husband, Nelson, and I were living in Great Falls, Virginia. She and I toured Europe and England for a month. She traveled with Elizabeth and Pete when they had their Winnebago. These travels took place in the winter when her little house in Maine was snowed in. She loved flying and visited Robert in Great Falls, Montana, and in Alaska.

Then Elizabeth and Pete bought a mobile home in Islamorada, Florida. That was their permanent winter home in Florida, and they owned a summer home in Hampton Beach. MCML would stay in her little house in Maine until the first part of October. Then Elizabeth and Pete put her on the plane in Boston and I picked her up in Washington, D.C. She would stay with Nelson and me at Great Falls until Thanksgiving, when I put her on the plane to Miami to stay with Elizabeth and Pete on the Keys until about March.

Then, with her satchels, she would land at the D.C. airport again. She would bid farewell to the captain, and he would salute, and she would salute back and say, "This is my 87th flight," or some number. One time as I eased her off the plane, she said to the captain, "That was a pretty rough landing, Cap'n." But she saluted him. He admitted it was.

Elizabeth and Pete would by that time have settled in to their place in

Hampton Beach. I would give them a breather. Then about June they would pick Mother up in Boston, and Elizabeth would clean out the spiders and mouse tracks from the house at Emery Mills, start the refrigerator and buy grub for her, and she was back alone in her own little house and loving it. She would get her '53 Chevy put in shape and go down to Springvale to get mail and food, traveling a sedate 25 miles an hour. Her license expired March 26, 1987, her 100th birthday.

As time went on, Mother had infirmities and bad spells, and a neighbor would notify Mike, Elizabeth and Pete's son, in New Castle, New Hampshire, and Elizabeth would fetch and carry and make appointments, etc. This would be in the summer. This pattern kept up for a long time.

Finally, in the summer of '86, Mother became ill when she was visiting Elizabeth in Hampton Beach. Elizabeth and I, with Robert's agreement, convinced MCML that selling her little house was the best thing to do. When she could travel, we took her down to Great Falls. Then she broke her ankle, and it was obvious that Elizabeth and I could not care for her day and night. I had visited a nursing home in Leesburg, Virginia, 20 miles from Great Falls, and in October of '86, we moved her there. Of course, she was unhappy there, couldn't understand the Southern way of talking, didn't like the food, roommate listened to us talk, no privacy, etc. I visited her about every day, took her smelly cheese, candy, Greek olives—all her loves. The home was a good one, with a hospital nearby. She walked around and got along well.

We planned a celebration of her 100th birthday, March 26, 1987, in the boardroom of the home. The crowning thing was Robert and Terry, his son, coming from Alaska. Many of our friends came. They knew Mary Lord, loved and admired her.

Now she was in her 101st year. She continued well and keen-minded. When the weather warmed up, I often pushed her in her wheelchair out on the grounds.

The day before she died, I visited and took her a letter from Robert. I rolled her as usual to the "meditation room" where we could be alone. She borrowed my glasses to read Robert's letter, and we talked. The next day she had a heart attack and died that evening.

During all these visits with me, she got great joy in relating incidents in her life: her childhood, descriptions of the house she lived in, her aunts and uncles and siblings, playmates and other people in Marblehead.

She had attended a commercial school in Boston by train every day, after high school. She was offered a job teaching commercial subjects in Springvale, Maine, and accepted it. She met Harold Lord that year. Her father thought she was too young to go so far away, so the next year she taught school in Marblehead. She and Harold visited back and forth. They became engaged and were married in 1910.

Mary and Harold Lord in Marblehead, 1915.

In her lifetime MCML knew and loved three children, four grandchildren, two step-grandchildren, four great-grandchildren and one great-great-granddaughter, as well as nieces, great-nieces and great-nephews. Now there is a great-great-grandson as well.

I KNEW I SHOULD HAVE been writing down all she told me, and at times I did. Once in the kitchen in Great Falls, I set up a tape recorder and began to ask leading questions. Away she went! But she became nettled by that microphone and quit. After that, I would grab whatever piece of paper was handy and scribble, at times asking her the spelling of some Marblehead name or place.

These incidents I write down are in no special order chronologically. Mother also had a way of placing herself in a good light in her adventures, even as you or I do. I wish now I had written down more of her memories.

Marblehead, Sept. 9, 1917: Linda Chapman, Edith May Mason, Martha Mason Lord,
Coralie Mason Litchman, Mary Cole Mason Lord, Elizabeth Ellen Lord.

ON THE FIRST FLOOR of their house on Mason Street, MCML's father had a small jeweler's shop. Her father called to her upstairs. "Mary, come down here and meet a friend of mine. His name is Mr. Britton. Say 'how-do-you-do.'"

She said, "Victor Britton
      Killed a kitten
      Hung it up to dry.
      Next day took it in
      And made a kitten pie."

In the late 1890s, there was a yacht club on Goodwin Court, where Stearns and McKay Yacht Yard used to be, called Bayview Yacht Club, and Uncle Henry Sparhawk was commodore. Around 1892, they were going to have a big fair at Abbot Hall and raffle off a doll. Grandmother Lamprell and Aunt Annie made the clothes for it. The winner had to sell the greatest amount of 10-cent ticket-votes. At the last day of the fair, the one with the most votes won. Mr. Clothey got votes for me—Mary Cole Mason. I went on the stage and got the doll. The dress was white dotted muslin, lace petticoat, pair of drawers with black lace, flannel petticoat, stockings, shoes and a blonde wig. I used to serve tea to the doll and my two imaginary friends, Lizzie Constant and Mrs. Butterfield.

Nat Rogers was the town honey-cart "operator." His job was to clean out privies. When he trundled by with his wagon, the kids would yell after him,

"Wherever you go
Wherever you git
You see Nat Rogers
Shoveling shit."

There were two sisters, Mrs. Soper and Mrs. Sinclair. They both walked with their heads down. One was called quarter of seven and the other half-past six, by the way they always carried their arms.

The Martin sisters wore hats that looked like upside-down bean pots. One was called Mayflower and the other Puritan.

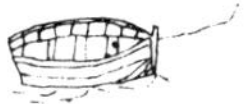

Captain Bill Gregory was a retired sea captain. He was a rough, hard-drinking, swearing guy. His brother, Captain Joseph Gregory, was just the opposite—polite and refined, and he lived with his mother on Summer Street. (He had a son, Lafayette, called Fayette Gregory, and *his* son was Ernest.) When I was teaching in the third-floor attic of the high school (the old Academy) on Pleasant Street, I could look down into the back yard of Joe Gregory's house on Summer Street. Every Wednesday at noontime I could see a hand organ man and his monkey playing for Mrs. Gregory. At that time, Joe had died and Mrs. Gregory was an old lady.

I could see down to Baker's Island, Manchester and Gloucester. Lovely view.

The red decanter with grapes and five small cups belonged to my mother's great-grandfather William Cole. He was a sea captain and brought the set home from London. His son, John, was cabin boy on his father's ship. He (Great-Uncle John) brought home the unstrung monkey beads. There were 48 for my mother, Elizabeth Ellen. Her sister, Sarah Abigail, was jealous of Lizzie, who had to give her sister 24. They came from Ceylon.

Fred L. Orne may not know it, but his high school teacher is alive and well, etc.

I think Fred was born in Pottsdam, New York. His mother was a Lindsey (Fred's middle name). His sister Madeline was unmarried, and a school

Left to right: Elizabeth Ann Clark, Elizabeth O'Brien and Mary Cole Mason "on the Float," Oct. 12, 1907.

teacher. Madeline was the oldest female descendant of James Mugford, a Revolutionary War hero. As Mugford died in Shirley Gut in Boston Harbor soon after he was married, he had no issue. When they came to name the U.S. ship after him, Madeline Orne was the oldest descendant. So her line was laterally developed as the one that received the silver service for christening U.S.S. Mugford. She kept it under her bed. *[The Dictionary of American Naval Fighting Ships lists two U.S.S. Mugfords, 1917 and 1935. MLG]*

Fred Orne was one of my pupils in shorthand and typing when I taught high school on Pleasant Street across from Nichols' Funeral Home. Also, I taught little Billy Martin arithmetic. This was around '07, '08, and '09—these three years. Fred had a brother, William. He was in my Sunday School class at the old North Church Congregational. Also in this class was one of the Humphrey twins, think it was Gordon. This class was in the Sunday School vestry. In back of me was another class, taught by the Superintendent of Town Schools, Almon Caswell. We used to call him "Kiss" after Kiss Caswell, who had a twitch. The Unitarian minister's name was Walkley and he looked like another of the town characters, so we called him after Red Frank from the shipyard, a driver of the honey cart. Walkley said, "These Marbleheaders . . . ," rolling his eyes up.

Captain Bill Gregory as an old man lived on the corner of Waldron and South streets. We four girls, Helen Paine and two others, were walking by on South Street. He stopped us—about '97—and said, "Come in, girls, and I'll sing you a song." He sat in a chair tilted back under a lilac bush. The walkway was edged with big rocks. We sat on the granite doorstep, and he leaned back and closed his eyes and began to sing sea chanteys. Then he said, "Girls, if you never go anywhere else before you die, go to Rio. It's the most beautiful place on earth." After more singing he opened his eyes and said, "You still here, girls?"

In the book *Sea Captains of Marblehead,* there was a good bit about the exploits of Cap'n Bill—even an added-on page about him *after* the book was published.

Down toward the depot from the Storey Grammar School was a small shop run by Mame and Jen (Mary and Jane) Davis. At recess, we would gather girls until we had 4 cents or 5 cents and go buy a cucumber pickle. They kept them in a great big hogshead. Floating in the brine were slices

Outside 2 Mason Street (right) where MCML was born: Mr. Coates at the wheel, with MCML, daughter Elizabeth and Herman Snow, in 1913.

of lemons and limes, and they were called by Mame and Jen "lemon flavored pickles." They would slice them for us and we would go back to school, juice running down our chins and arms. The cukes were, seems like, a foot long, over-ripe cukes with *big seeds*. The sisters wouldn't sell any pickles until they had soaked in the concoction a certain length of time. Wow! Were they good. Mame and Jen were dwarfs—known nowadays as "little people."

Lucy Brown, whose father's name was Osawatomie Brown, was the cause of my not getting vaccinated. Lucy lived on Linden Street. At that time, my father was on the school board along with Thomas W. Tucker, the Reverend van der Pyl, Dr. Eveleth, Edith G. Fabens and two others. The law said every child must be vaccinated. Among others, Father did not believe in injecting serum from a cow, from an animal, into a healthy person, but Mother did believe in vaccination. On this day she told my older sister Bess (Martha Betsy) to take me to Dr. Eveleth to get a vaccination. The doctor lived at that time in the Robie Mansion at the top of Darling Street. This was a short distance from our house, which was across from the Lee Mansion at the foot of Mason Street. As we got to the door of the doctor's office, we could hear a commotion, yelling and screaming, inside. The doctor opened the door and said, "Tell Lee (my mother) I can't do it now. I'm busy. Tell her to send you back tomorrow." Beyond him we could see on the floor Lucy Brown thrashing around. We turned around and went home. Bess announced, "Dr. Eveleth is busy with Lucy Brown. She's having a fit." Later, Father said, "That settles it. Mary will have no vaccination." So, between Dr. Eveleth and Isaac Wyman Mason, Jr., there was an understanding, and I wasn't vaccinated until I went to Europe with my daughter Martha in 1960, when I was 73 years old. *[She had it on her thigh, by her choice. MLG]*

There was another store which carried wonderful pickles. That was in Mr. Rogers' place in Townhouse Square. He kept his in a small keg which contained pickled limes. After the limes were sold, Mrs. Rogers would take any fresh oranges with bad places, cut out the places and put the sound parts in the pickled lime juice. There were two kegs going, one for soaking and one ready to sell. "Keep away from that keg, girls! They're not ready yet!" she would say. She had a dipper.

In back of Rogers' store was the alley, where we used to shortcut to the Mugford School on Mechanic Street, the second and third grades—teachers Maria L. Martin, second, and Suzannah Goodwin, third. The High Street School had third and fourth grades, Harriet Prichard and Amy P. Doe, teachers. Another shortcut alley was on Washington Street, across from Peach's store. It went up to High Street, nothing but solid ledge. (Hamlin had the store before Peach.)

Tax bills were long, like handbills, and had to be written by hand. My sister Cora and Father were the only ones to write the tax bills, as they had the most legible hand.

The streets were stacked by sides—even numbers on one pile, odd numbers on another. For instance, I would take Reed's Hill area, which included Abbot, Bowden, Jefferson, Sewall, Reed, Mt. Vernon, Linden, Guernsey and Jersey streets and Highland Terrace.

I would start out in the morning with a pile of tax bills in a basket. The bill was to be given to a person whose name was on it or to someone in

THE OLD SPITE HOUSE, MARBLEHEAD, MASS.
43593

that household. All those not delivered on one day were taken back the next day. Most people were home in those days—nowhere else to go.

The assessors—three of them—would pass the tax books to my father about the first of July. After they were written by Father or my sister, they would be stacked all over the house by streets. Tax bills everywhere!

These were the long streets: Jersey (at that time, Jersey went as far as Allen Lindsey's house), Washington, Pleasant, Front, Green, Elm (including Back Street), Gregory, Lee and Atlantic Avenue. Clifton suburb started around where the Glover School is now. That was called the farm district.

All year-round residents were given tax bills by some of our family, who walked to each house to deliver them. Non-residents were mailed their tax bills, including the Neck and Peach's Point. But any year-round residents were handed their tax bills—like the Barrys of Peach's Point and the Goodwins at Naugus Head and Goodwin's Landing.

On discount nights, which went way into November, Father would come home down the hill at 2 or 3 o'clock in the morning with very much cash, which he would distribute all over the attic for safety. We girls slept in the attic and he would wake me up when he did so, and when I asked him what was the matter, he would say, "Nothing. Go back to sleep."

One morning after a discount night, he asked me to take a big amount of money down the street to the Grand Bank in a paper bag and give it to Everett Paine, who was Town Treasurer. He thought by my taking it to the bank I would not be stopped and robbed. Our house had no locks on the windows, and the doors could be opened with a skeleton key. My mother wanted a policeman to come home with my father at night, but he would have none of that. He would be alone in his office in Abbot Hall almost all night working on the books.

Once I went with Mr. Coates, a neighbor, to visit the Revenue Cutter "Dexter"—Captain Sill—in the harbor. I was attended by a Filipino boy while Mr. Coates transacted business with the captain. I was seasick. I was so embarrassed!

Three of us girls, Alice Litchman, Elviry Snellen and I, walked across the frozen-over harbor with a man who was drunk. The ice would go up and

Marblehead, Mass. Frozen Harbor

ABBOTT HALL, FROM ROCKAWAY STREET, MARBLEHEAD, MASS.

down with the waves. It was just before supper, and somehow my brother
Jot (Jonathan) and Father had heard about it before I got home. I got the
dickens for that.

We played dolls in front of the painting "Spirit of '76" in the reading
room of Abbot Hall. We also played dolls in the belfry. Sometimes we used
dead birds as dolls. It was a terrible noise when the clock struck the hour.

We had a play house in our back yard. My brother Jot's gang of young
men used it as a clubhouse at night—The Doggers, they called themselves.
One night they had a fire on the roof. It started from an over-stuffed stove.
Had to have the fire department.

At about 1919, there were two colored families in Marblehead—the
Fountains, on Stacey Street, and the Bakers, on the corner of Middle and
South, the flatiron building. Mr. and Mrs. Fountain's son, on Glover Street,

had Marian, Gladys and about four others—a nice family. The Bakers had Wesley, Ida and Kate. Wesley was older and a nice young man, and Ida was always trying to keep Kate down and behave herself. Mrs. Baker was always hanging out the window yelling and telling the children what to do. Kate was like her mother and didn't give a darn for anybody. Mrs. Baker was very nice.

Kate grew up and married out of town. She had a daughter about the age of Martha. One time when all the Lords were visiting Marblehead, Fred Litchman, who was always on the lookout for interesting picture possibilities, asked me if Martha could pose with Kate's daughter. I said sure. Kate took her girl home for a dressing-up and so did I, and the resulting pictures were very good. "Maybe Mary will mind," said Kate. "Of course not," said Uncle Fred.

In the Revolutionary War there was a peddler named Isaac Wyman who made lots of money selling provisions, clothing, etc., to the soldiers. He became very rich and took a promissory note for $60,000 to the Continental Congress to help the war effort.

Mr. Wyman, then 70, took a liking to my great-grandfather, Jonathan

Mary and Kate's daughters, February 1920.

Breed Mason, born in Salem in 1792. Jonathan's wife, Martha Doliber Severy, was pregnant. Mr. Wyman said if the baby was a boy and they named him after him, Wyman, he would make the boy a total heir. It was a boy, and they named him Isaac Wyman Mason.

But in three years, Isaac Wyman married Elizabeth Smith, a barmaid in Salem, about 18. He had three children, Isaac Chauncy Wyman and Susan Wyman and one other. So my grandfather Isaac Wyman Mason didn't inherit anything.

[MCML's paternal grandmother, Lydia Ann Dennis, married Isaac Wyman Mason, Sr., born 1822. They had I.W. Mason, Jr., MCML's father, born in 1849.

[In the 1920s, MCML's sister Martha Betsy Mason went to Dermot, Arkansas, in the Ozarks for a vacation and visited the town of Wyman, named after "a mine owner near Boston." MLG]

On the 30th of May or the nearest Friday, each local GAR (Grand Army of the Republic) Civil War veteran member was assigned a school to visit to talk to the children about the late great war, and patriotism.

Thomas W. Swazey had the high school, Osawatomie Brown had another.

We sang "Columbia the Gem of the Ocean," "Maryland, My Maryland" and "Just Before the Battle, Mother." The men had put flags on each soldier's grave the day before.

We girls were 10 or 11 years old, and we took it upon ourselves to help. This was the season of lilacs, peonies and jonquils, and we gathered all our neighborhoods would give us. Up through Bassets Lane, then Jersey (as far as Nat Lindsey's house), cut across the field into a new part of the cemetery looking for GAR flags with no flowers. We kneeled down, said a prayer, left flowers and went on to the next grave. Every time I hear robins singing and smell lilacs and peonies, I remember that spring day with birds flying in the sunshine.

My grandmother Sallie Ashton High Cole Lamprell (first husband, Samuel Horton Cole, Sr.; second, William Andrews Lamprell. Clear?)—well, Sallie read tea leaves.

Sallie Ashton High Cole Lamprell, born in Marblehead, Feb. 18, 1826.

Grandmother and Grandfather Cole went to Rehobeth Beach for a visit. Aunt Becker (Great-Aunt Rebecca) Mullet, Grandmother's youngest sister, came to take care of the children. Evidently she hated to cook or was lazy, for all she fed the kids was hasty pudding—cornmeal mush covered with milk and molasses. It went through the kids like a shot and left them sore.

Ellen Bowden, who lived at the Agnes Surriage Well house, was engaged to John High, my grandmother Sallie Ashton High Cole Lamprell's oldest brother. They had a quarrel, and he said he was going to leave Marblehead and never return. He did, and no one knew of his whereabouts and he never wrote to any of them.

When the Flying Cloud made her record trip from New York to San Francisco with Josiah P. Cressey as master (left New York June 3, 1851—89 days, 21 hours; second trip, 1854—89 days, 8 hours), all the country was waiting for the vessel to finish the trip. On the ship was a cabin boy by the name of John Whidden. He lived in the Glover Mansion and as a boy used to hang around the wharves. When the vessel was sighted coming through the Golden Gate, a large crowd gathered on the wharves there to welcome her. The men on board were given leave and landed on the wharf. Of course, John Whidden went also. While in the crowd he noticed a man who looked to him like John High. He spoke to him and said, "I know you. You are John High who left Marblehead." The man said, "You must be mistaken. I am not the man you spoke of." The boy tried to get some of the men from the vessel, but when he turned around the man had disappeared into the crowd. When the boy sailed back to Marblehead he told all of the people he met about the man. He was certain he was John High, as he had seen him many times on the wharf at home.

Rebecca High was a baby when her brother John, as the oldest, used to play with her on the floor. She was his favorite. She grew up and was married to a man by the name of Mullet. She had four children. Her husband died, and she was very poor. She lived in the old High house on Front Street next to the Leslie Hotel (the old Coffin house). The two-story-and-a-half house, with the front door facing south, was partway out into the street. Upstairs were Great-Uncle Bill and Aunt Sarah. One night when it was dark, there was a knock on the door of the ell (parallel to the harbor), which was the kitchen. Rebecca took the lantern to the door and held it up. "Who is it?" she said.

A strange man said, "What is your name?"

She was a very timid woman but told him what he wanted to know.

"May I have a drink of water?" he asked, smiling all the while. He stepped down into the kitchen and went right over to the water pail and took a dipper of water, then said good night to her and left. It was pitch dark, but he went around the end of the ell and down the steep cliff to Homan's Beach. She heard him get into a dory and could hear him row out into the harbor. The night before there had come into the roadstead after dark a large vessel and anchored between the Fort and the lighthouse. The men on shore, thinking the vessel might be putting in for overnight, expected someone

would come ashore in the morning. But in the morning the ship was gone, and no one ever knew what ship she was nor where she hailed from.

I like to think, although I have nothing to go on, that before the man went to the High house he might have gone to Orne Street and perhaps peeked into the window of Ellen Bowden's house.

Doubtless the man was John High and wanted to see the old places once more.

I remember the old house. There was no sidewalk, and when anyone passed by the windows, which were right on the street, you could put your hand, if the windows were open, right on to Great-Aunt Rebecca's bed. The

kitchen in the ell was one step down from the street, and the water pail and dipper were always right on the bench in the corner of the room. So when the man stepped down into the kitchen in the dark he must have known where the pail was.

Ellen never married. She was a pal of my grandmother. I have a picture that Uncle Will Broughton took. I think it must have been near the year of 1895. Ellen and Grandmother are sitting on a large rock, and there are several persons around them. It was a picnic and was on Brown's Island in Barnegat.

My great-grandfather William Cole sighted a shipwreck and rescued a man, wife and child. He brought them into Marblehead. Man's name was Samuel Horton. Everyone liked the little family. Several people named their children after Samuel Horton.

William's wife had a boy and named him Samuel Horton Cole. Mrs. Pitman married a Brown and had a boy and named him Samuel Horton

Brown. *He* had a son, Samuel Horton Brown, Jr.

The high bureau Martha has now belonged to Samuel Horton Cole, Sr.

The Colemans, across from Rockaway Street, always needed coal during the winter. John S. Martin's wagon delivered. He backed his wagon up the drive beside the house right to the cellar window, and that made the horse come out over the sled tracks. Kids slid down the hill and under the belly of the horse, whose only reaction was twitching ears. The driver, Red Frank, would shake his fist and swear at us kids.

John S. Martin's coal supply came by collier to his wharf up near the Electric Light Plant. The other coal companies were Humphrey & Twisden, at the end of Water Street, and Gilbert and Cole, on Bessom Street. Coal came by train and ship.

Aunt Ruth Lane could charm off warts and lived on the corner of Elm (Back), next to the corner of Elm and Cowell. Aunt Ruth Swett lived on

Beacon Street, at the bottom of the hill as it turns. She was old and belonged to the Congo Church.

Mother's lady friends who belonged to different churches vied with each other to take me to concerts, prayer meetings and recitals. I was 4, 5, 6 years old and was cute and interested in everything.

There was a prayer meeting at Crocker Park every Sunday in the late afternoon. They used to keep the little organ in Snellen's barn, at the left going up from Front Street. The organ was taken out in a little tip cart and carried onto the grass. Albert Pierce played the bugle. Frank Broughton ran the meeting. I went with Mrs. Coates. We sat on benches under the bandstand. It sounded lovely—people in the harbor in boats could hear. A crowd was always there singing and standing.

In the morning on Sunday as a child, I went to Sunday School in the Baptist Church. In the afternoon I went with Carrie Rogers, Mrs. Coates' sister.

Lyddy Bowden lived at the site of the Old Fountain Inn, where the Agnes Surriage well was. Lyddy's house was built facing the Fort. I sat on the grass.

Harbor from Crocker Park, MARBLEHEAD, Mass.

Marblehead, Mass. - Harbor from Crocker Park.

A lovely view. Then home in time to go with Mrs. Coates to prayer meeting on the Head (Crocker Park). Carrie said, "Mary was a damned handsome bitch." She had a good heart but used to swear a blue streak.

Lewis Doane was an old boyfriend [*of MCML's*]. He went to Deane Academy and Tufts. A girl made fudge and put it in her desk in high school. Lewis sat in her seat in the next class, found the box and finished the fudge. We called him Fudgie.

Frank Brown had a meat market across from Summer Street and next to Dolly Doane's. Frank had three children—Fred, Ambrose and Pearl. Fred had a big sled named "Half Rock." Ellsworth Fleet had a big sled named "Jumbo." They raced from Abbot Hall, down around Darling Street and sometimes down to Ferry Lane, aka Tucker's Lane.

There was a big signboard at the top of Darling Street against the Chinese laundry. Florence Martin was visiting the Cloutmans on the corner of Lookout Court and was on one sled. As it turned the corner on Darling Street, Florence was thrown off the sled against the signboard and broke her leg. Dr. Eveleth came right away—his office was in the Robey Mansion.

Frank Brown's wife was very fat.

These are some stores when I was a girl:

Let's start with Sco Bowden's (William Scobie) on Hooper Street, almost at the end, facing Tucker. General stuff. Grandfather Mason (Isaac Wyman Mason, Sr.) had a store halfway up Mason Street. General stuff. Mr. Smith's store was at 162 Washington Street. The family lived upstairs. On the corner, selling tea and coffee, was Mr. Marshall. I was sent with a tea coupon to get a chamber pot. I didn't like to carry a pot on the street.

From the Grand Bank was Horace Sweet's funeral parlor. Next, a meat shop. Then Homan's ice cream, and the Atkins drug store. Then Rogers' fruit store. Across from the top of Darling Street was a Chinese laundry, next a barber, then Melzard's candy store, and then Nat Snow's. Mr. Freeto's newspaper shop. Next, Jim Buzzell's house, 2½-story. Frank Brown's store. Then a barn sat in back of Doane's, and then the Doanes' home.

Then Doane's Plumbing, Langley's Meat Shop, then the big Mugford Building with Salkins and Laskey's clothing store with a ballroom on top. Then Trasher's candy store. Then where later was Prue Snow and her father's art gallery. Then Goodwin's Drug Store, the home of Judge Storey. Next a grass plot. Then Billy Lemon's home. Downstairs in the front room was Shepards Drug Store. William Shepard and family lived in back, and the Lemons lived upstairs. Mr. Russell used to sell his pickled limes on a cart there. Then two big buildings against each other—the first was Arrington's Hardware and joining was Cloon's Hardware. Then came State Street.

In the War of 1812, or thereabouts, one of our vessels, Navy, was in Valparaiso, Chile, harbor. There was an epidemic of typhus going on, and the American crew helped out. Lieutenant Cowell caught the disease and died. He was buried in that city.

Our Navy wanted a gunboat named after him. As Cowell was unmarried, a female descendant had to christen the boat. Laterally, Emma Garney, a sour old maid who lived with her brother on Watson Street, was the only one they dug up. She used to chase the kids off her edge of lawn on their way to school.

We would take the knockabout "Milo" (sailboat) in the late 1890s and anchor off Manchester, near Norman's Woe. A small island was overgrown with wild elderberries. The Milo towed a punt which we rowed ashore, filled with berries and took back out to the Milo. Then we sailed home and carried the fruit in clothes baskets to the house, dipped the bunches of berries in water in a wooden tub, stripped off the berries and mashed them. Simmered 'til they burst, and let them drain in a bag. Then they made wine—don't know how.

Kids could have a tiny bit when they came in from skating or sliding in winter. When Mother had the "girls" down, she served wine. There were

Emma Woodfin, Emma Shedd and Carrie and Lil Potter. Had fruitcake along with it.

Ella Woodfin put a rotten pear in Mary Lou Chamberlain's seat in school (Spring Street School—Miss Graves, teacher). She sat down, and a funny look came over her face. "Mary Lou, what's the matter?" asked Miss Graves. "Somebody has done a terrible thing," faltered Mary Lou. She was nasty nice.

Ella Woodfin's father was a blacksmith near school at the top of the hill on what is now Guernsey Street. He was known as Uncle Bug. Mary Lou married John Broughton.

Next to Abbot Hall on the height of land is Lookout Court overlooking the harbor. The old houses there were built on rocks—square colonial houses with lookout walks on their roofs. These places had a view of the ocean across the harbor and the Neck, and the family could get the first glimpse of a returning ship. Each ship had a rigging that was familiar to seamen,

Marblehead High School, fall 1901. MCML is the second girl from the right, front row.

and a returning ship could be recognized by its silhouette.

Grandmother Mason lived in one of these houses. The cellar kitchen looked out and down over the rocks. It was the sunny side. Blue painted paneling, long windows overlooking the harbor. Small old-fashioned garden —heliotrope, lady delights, peonies, lily of the valley, bleeding heart, violets, a lilac tree—cobblestones marking paths—low fence on the street side. Large old dory filled with flowers. Quince and apple and cherry trees. And the outdoor shen-ary-gon (privy) with a view. Owned also the next house on the corner of Waldron and Gregory streets. I used to undress in the cellar —run across the street—down over the rocks to Jimmie Lane's Cove (First) and go bathing with about a dozen other children. Wore old calico dress.

Grandmother and Grandfather Cole "went around with" another couple who lived on Waldron Court—in their early married life—William Andrews Lamprell and wife Anne Goldthwaite. She lost her child at birth and went demented.

One night she went from home. They hunted around the neighborhood. All the men searched both First and Second coves. Couldn't find her. My grandfather suggested going to the well which was down in the garden towards what is now Atlantic Avenue. She had jumped in the well; and when the lantern was held below, the light glinted on her glasses. There she was, drowned. My grandfather climbed down the ladder and brought her up.

After my grandfather Cole died, my grandmother married Mr. Lamprell, although I never saw him. He died before I was born. I have a beaten gold brooch which belonged to Anne Lamprell before she was married. I had an aunt who was named for her—Annie Lamprell Cole, who married Henry Clarence Sparhawk after whom my brother Henry was named when he was born in 1890. I, Mary Cole Mason Lord, was born in 1887.

Sarah Abigail Cole Wadden, my oldest aunt, had a sickness when a baby which left her with one crippled leg which was shorter than the other. She was very proud and very spoiled.

Uncle John High Cole married Eliza Brown. She died in her late nineties. They had 15 children, of which eight grew up.

John High, Jr., served on the Constitution in the War of 1812. His wife, Betsy High, petitioned the government for help for destitute widows and

MCML's mother, Elizabeth Ellen Cole Mason.

Sisters Coralie Mason Litchman and Mary Cole Mason Lord.

children of Marblehead, Massachusetts.

Captain Steward was master of the Constitution at that time, and Hull was commodore. John High, Jr., was also captain of his own ship, "Betsy." The ivory miniature painting of Captain High was made in Nantes, France, before the War of 1812.

Uncle Sam, my mother's brother, married Mary Goodwin (after whom I was named), and they lived on Goodwin's Court off Front Street. I used to go there for dinner (noon) every Sunday after Sunday School. Mother always coached me on a poem to recite after dinner—"to pay for what I ate," Uncle Sam used to say.

One week we ran out of poems, so Mother said to recite a poem that I had said before and give it another title. But Uncle Sam caught me—but he gave me the customary dime. Aunt Mary would say, "Sam, don't tease the child."

Uncle Sam and I after dinner would go to Goodwin's Head and sit on the rocks and enjoy the harbor view. Aunt Mary died when I was in the fourth grade, and I was unconsolable because I loved her and missed her.

Uncle Sam was a butcher and had a store on South Street. One day, my mother sent me there to get an "aitch bone" (the rump bone, as of beef). Uncle Sam said, "How do you spell it?" I couldn't. So he said, "Then you can't have it." I went home without it, and Father put me to hunting in the dictionary for the spelling. Then up I went again for the meat.

I got burned by touching the Magee iron range. Grecian heads were embossed on my bottom.

We enjoyed Aunt Ide's home at Barnegat. Uncle Will Broughton was a perfect host. We swam there when the tide was in. No surf. And plenty of fun. Sometimes we walked to Aunt Ide's, and again we would row from Quiner's Wharf, around the Fort to Barnegat. In the spring, we would gather the hearts of sweet flag there and in the fall the sticky buds of Balm of Gilead tree, from which Mother made salve for cuts and burns.

Also we would gather wild cherries on Village Street. Mother would put sugar and alcohol and mash them, then strain it. It was a good remedy for "summer complaint."

CORINTHIAN YACHT CLUB, MARBLEHEAD NECK
PUBLISHED BY LOUIS A. ARDELL, MARBLEHEAD, MASS.

All summer we were on the water—sailing, rowing, etc. Another girl and I would swipe a dory. Take along two umbrellas with crook handles. Then we would row up to the upper end of the harbor, hook the umbrellas to the bow or stern thwarts and sail down harbor, playing with our dolls and I steering with an oar. When we got to the lighthouse, we would row back and do it all over again, going between the palatial yachts. No motor boats then. Sometimes the chefs on the yachts would hand out food to us.

On Bartoll's Head (Crocker Park), I had a favorite cubby-hole of a rock on which I played house. At high tide I had to hold up my legs so I would not get wet.

The whole family would go sailing, leaving food on the back of the stove to keep warm. Mother would fix up a quick lunch and away we would go. We had wonderful fish fries on Eagle Island—sail to the island in the Milo, anchor, row ashore, build a fire, catch fish and have a fry.

On the beach at Castle Rock, there was a large flat rock we used as a table.

And the band concerts! Monday evening at the Corinthian Yacht Club and Thursday at the Eastern Y.C. More fun!

My two brothers Ernest and Henry, out sailing, used to tease me and try to make me seasick and then I would "throw." But Jot, my other brother, would give me something to do, like tending the sheet or steering, and I was OK and was never seasick when I went sailing with him.

The whole family went sailing on the Bonita and the Milo—it seems as if we were on the water all summer. The Milo was the last boat to be pulled up in the fall at Quiner's Wharf and the first in the spring to go in the water.

I can smell that wonderful smell now—oakum, varnish, paint, salt water, etc. It was fascinating to watch the men working on the boats.

Charles Wentworth Lord, father of my husband, Harold, was born in 1848 in Lebanon, Maine. His mother was Betsy Wentworth, who married a Corson first, then Eli Ball Lord. Betsy's father was Seth Wentworth. Betsy's sister, Mary, married a Colbath, whose brother was Jeremiah Colbath from Farmington, New Hampshire. Jeremiah got into politics, changed his name to Henry Wilson, and served in U.S. Grant's first administration as vice president.

[In the Maine Antique Digest of December 1991 was an item of historical

On the side steps of the Lee Mansion, 1917: Flanked by Linda Chapman (left) and Mabel Jordan in uniforms—possibly Red Cross—are Fred and Coralie Litchman and Harold and Mary Lord (back row) and Harold's sister Florence, from Springvale, Maine, with Elizabeth and Martha Lord.

interest. Included in Richard A. Bourne's auction of Nov. 30, 1991, was the following:

["Rare and important gold-headed cane presented to the Honorable Henry Wilson by 'Friends in California,' an Overland Stagecoach with inlay of gold matrix on the end (Henry Wilson was vice president under Ulysses S. Grant)."

[I, Martha, looked up Henry Wilson in the dictionary, and by golly, there he was; and after his name was in parenthesis Jeremiah Jones Colbath. So much for MCML's memory. MLG]

[My Grandfather Lord had two sisters, Caroline and Lucy. Lucy married Charles Pray of Salmon Falls, New Hampshire, and had no children. Caroline invited her boyfriend to meet her family. Her father, Eli Ball Lord, shouted, "Never! No one with that name shall ever join my family!" Caroline never married and "died young of a broken heart." I don't know what the name was that had such an effect.

[Grandfather Charles Wentworth Lord had a brother Henry who married "Aunt Lizzie" and lived in Springvale, Maine. MLG]

URBAN AND SUBURBAN NEWS

MARBLEHEAD.

Ninety Years Old Today.

The oldest citizen of Marblehead, Isaac W. Mason, is today observing his 90th birthday at his home on Mason street, and although not in the best of health, he was able to receive the congratulations of his friends and extend greetings to his family.

Mr. Mason is a native of Marblehead, having been born here March 8, 1822, his parents being Jonathan B. and Martha Mason, who were also natives of the town. The grandfather of Mr. Mason, William Mason, came to America from the island of Guernsey, in the English channel, and in company with his two brothers, Joseph and John, first landed in Boston on March 11, 1714. Jonathan B. Mason, father of Mr. Mason, was an old Marblehead sea captain and was a prisoner at one time in Dartmoor prison in England.

Isaac W. Mason was the youngest of six children, and when five years of age attended the private school on Summer street taught by Miss Rebecca Bliss on the present site of the Wyman house, and later entered the public schools in the old Town House.

Four Generations of the Mason Family of Marblehead.
Left to right—Warren Mason, Ernest C. Mason, Isaac W. Mason Jr., Isaac W. Mason, who is celebrating 90th anniversary of his birth today.

The P

The Parkland banquet at the George F. Vinc last evening. Day, Ralph B Kennet Day an entertained w stories. The by violin sol piano solos those prese Ralph Day cent, Roy Albert Hi son, all

SHA
Some

It spea the in Gh to lo p li i h a

At the age of 10 years he went on a sea trip to New York with his father as cook on the schooner Mechanic, under Captain Edmund Kimball.

The trip to New York was an eventful one in the life of Mr. Mason, for while in New York harbor he saw the wreck of the Clermont, Robert Fulton's first steamboat, the first craft to move in the world under steam power. While in New York he also saw workmen lay the foundation of the Astor house, which was to become one of the most celebrated hotels in the entire country. On his return trip to Marblehead the ports of New London and New Haven were visited, the schooner reaching Marblehead in September, 1833.

While still a youth Mr. Mason made seven trips to the Grand Banks in the schooner Crescent under Skipper [George] Pierce. On one of the trips to the Grand Banks Mr. Mason met with an accident which has handicapped him throughout his entire life. In the midst of a heavy fog, a large vessel bore down upon the small fishing schooner, and in blowing a foghorn, Mr. Mason broke the ear drum of his right ear and injured the left ear in ⋯⋯able to

When Grandma Garvin died, whom Nana Lord was caring for, it was in the fall of 1911. Nana's children persuaded her to go out to California to visit her sons, Edward and Frank. When she returned east in June 1912, there was a gala chicken dinner on a Sunday at Pleasant Street in Springvale, Maine, to welcome her home. The Portland folks—Florence, Harry, Herman and Mabel—came home, and Harold and I and Elizabeth, who was then 7 months old, were there, too. We made a freezer of ice cream which was put down cellar to "ripen."

In the middle of dinner the fire alarm blew. The fire was at the print works at the mill on the river. It was a hot day with a strong wind, which blew from the fire up the slope and along Pleasant Street, dropping burning cinders on roofs.

I had put Elizabeth upstairs for her nap.

They sent Herman upstairs to climb through the scuttle (a skylight to the roof) to spot any burning places. At the same time, firemen arrived and ran upstairs, through a bedroom and out the window to get to the kitchen roof. They came down and said, "Hey, do you know there is a baby in a room upstairs?" "Yes, I know," said I. "That is my daughter." The men said, "She's not crying—just watching us run by the bed and out the window and back again." We were told to pack things in trunks and take them out of the house. All the houses along the street did the same.

When the danger was over, we brought in the trunks, and one had nothing in it but a man's straw hat! Then we came in and had the ice cream.

such a manner that he has been una[ble to] hear any but the loudest noise. After making seven trips to the Grand Banks, Mr. Mason gave up sea life and settled down in Marblehead to manufacture shoes, and for many years engaged in that industry. He retired from active work some years ago.

"Old Ike," as he is familiarly called, is known by nearly every inhabitant of Marblehead, and as the owner of Mason's Rocks he will always be remembered, for in spite of scores of offers to purchase the property by summer residents, he declares his intention of holding them always and to keep them at the disposal of the general public as long as he lives.

Mr. Mason has one son, Isaac W. Mason Jr., the present tax collector of the town, and six grandchildren, Harbormaster Ernest C. Mason, Jonathan B. Mason, Henry C. Mason, Miss Betsey Mason, Mrs. Fred B. Litchman and Mrs. Harold K. Lord, besides six great-grandchildren.

MCML and baby Elizabeth.

Henry F. Pitman lived up at Naugus Head farm at Marblehead. He had six daughters. Mary, the oldest, married a Goldthwaite; one married Ben Lindsay, one married Amos Graves, on the corner of Basset and Washington; one married James Graves, a captain in the Civil War whose fellow soldier was Captain Stewart McClearn (they built identical houses side by side beyond the track). One married a Wilkins on Abbot Street; and the sixth was Elizabeth, who married Samuel Horton Brown. The Pitman land was divided up.

One of Amos Graves' daughters married Henry Brown, brother of Samuel Horton (above). Henry lived on the corner of Pickett Street in the old Pedrick house. One of the rooms was papered with money printed for the Civil War.

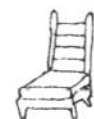

Edith and Bertha Graves came down by trolley to high school from the Lynn Road farms. The Alleys, Hoopers and Pecks also sent children to high school, and they came very early. Also, the Draytons, whose father took care of the lighthouse—Henry and William—and four more rowed across harbor from the Corinthian Yacht Club.

Edith's father gave her a gold watch to take to Mr. Cook, the jeweler, to be fixed. She hung her coat in the girls' entry and left the watch in the pocket.

Mr. John B. Graves was janitor, a fine man—came early to stoke up the furnace. Edith went to get her coat—and no watch. Mr. Campbell called a meeting. Everyone searched, children and teachers. No watch.

In time the furor died down. Outside the attic schoolroom, my room, was the open attic where all sorts of culch—books, paper, furniture—was stored and piled up. I went to get paper there, and there was a taken-apart watch. After a while, Bill Drayton confessed.

Of the painting of the baby, Martha Mason No. 5, owned now by Leslie Lord Roth of Kenai, Alaska, MCML said, "She was born two years after her brother, Isaac Wyman Mason, Jr., my father. Her parents were I.W. Mason, Sr., and Lydia Ann Dennis Mason, born 1825.

"Lydia woke in the middle of the night and saw a light source that shone in the room. She said, 'That is a kind of omen. Someone is going to pass on.' They woke and the baby was dead in her cradle. The painting was done in September; and shortly after, she died, when she was 9 months old."

L. A. W

M
CML ALWAYS SAID she believed in cremation and wanted it for herself.
After all, her father, Isaac Wyman Mason, Jr., was the first to be cremated
in the new Salem crematorium, in 1918.

When she passed away on June 15, 1988, Elizabeth, Robert and I, Martha,
made plans to carry out Mother's wishes. We knew she loved the ocean, the
North Atlantic. So when we could arrange to get together—the right ocean,
boat, Sunday, family members and Mother's ashes—in New Hampshire, we
gathered at Michael's house at New Castle, all but Robert. The date was
Sunday, August 14, 1988.

Michael, Elizabeth and Pete's son, lives a stone's throw from the
Piscataqua River as it forms the boundary between Maine and New Hampshire,
passes Portsmouth and reaches the sea. He has a roomy lobster-type boat
and loves fishing. Elizabeth and Pete were at their trailer in Hampton Beach,
New Hampshire, for the summer, and Nelson and I planned our trip from
Great Falls, Virginia. The Unitarian Church in Sanford, Maine, where Mother
had been a member, had been notified, along with newspapers in Washington,
D.C., and Portland, Maine.

The chosen Sunday was sultry, hazy and humid. Mike's wife, Jo, carried
a cooler with iced soda. The six of us had to make two trips in Mike's skiff

to his boat anchored just offshore. The Sunday boaters were streaming out
of harbor, past the Navy Yard to open sea, dodging buoys and each other.
There were long greasy swells which changed to chop. In the west were
banked ominous dark clouds.

As we neared the Portsmouth Light buoy, Mike said, "Is this all right,
Mother?" Elizabeth and I looked at each other and nodded. Mike cut the
engine. I took out the heavy plastic bag, tore open the end, and slid the
light gray, fine ashes into the water. Elizabeth and I cried silently. The wind
and waves tossed the boat and carried the stream away from us. Mike said
quietly, "First time I ever chummed with my grandmother." We broke into
laughter through tears. Jo passed the soda cans, and we all raised a salute
to Mary. She would have loved it.

Michael revved up the boat and sailed around the Fort on the point and
into the salt water creeks where folks have their homes, docks and boats.
He steered back around through Sagamore Creek, by the Hotel Wentworth
and under the short bridges that connect the islands which are New Castle.
Mother always loved this trip through these deep waterways.

The cloud bank loomed higher, so Mike made a run for it, bucking the
current by the Navy Yard and dodging the craft racing to safety. Jo caught

the buoy, Mike levered us old folks into the skiff, made two trips to the beach and just made it up to the house through big drops. The men went out for lobster rolls, and we toasted Mary again.

Back in Sanford, the church had offered their kitchen and large room for a gathering of Mary's friends and those who knew her from her days at the hospital. So two days later, on Aug. 16, 1988, we gathered again: Nelson and I, Elizabeth and Pete, Mike and Jo, and Brianna Mason Perl—MCML's new great-great-grandchild—and her mother, Nicole Armitage Perl, daughter of Mike and Jo. Several old friends of Mother's brought ice, made tea, set up the tables and spread tablecloths, cookies and flowers. There were some of my high school friends and neighbors of Mother's. We sat in a sort of circle. The minister was there and watched this loving remembrance time. Even an old boyfriend of mine came. The minister said a short benediction and we cleaned up. (This boyfriend was not the one I knew in '35-'36 who went to Harvard and came to see me in Sanford, where I did my first teaching. He was enthralled by Mother and once said, "I would marry you so I could have your mother for a mother-in-law!")

In our living room in Great Falls was a recording player piano, a 6-foot grand that we kept for a pianist-conductor friend, Tim Rowe. Each winter in the early 1980s, Tim's piano students gave a recital for parents and friends, and MCML was an appreciative listener. "And here is Mrs. Lord again," Tim announced one year. "She was alive while Tchaikowsky was alive!" Turning to Mother, he said, "And when were you born, again, Mrs. Lord?" In a clear, positive voice, she said, "I'm not a born-again. I'm a Unitarian."

Every grownup roared with laughter, and the recital began. Afterward I asked Mother if she knew what "born again" meant. "Sure," she said. "Jimmy Carter was a born-again."

From her father, Ike, MCML got her love of words and their use, and the need for accuracy in spelling and pronunciation. One of her duties in the hospital was taking down the patients' histories and treatment. Of course, many of the doctors were younger than she was, but they called her Mary and wanted her to be their transcriber. They knew she could spell and keep information to herself, which is a good thing in a small town (or anywhere).

She was taking down, in her early-1900s shorthand only she could read,

Sunday Afternoon Dec. 27, 1981

We had the AARP Christmas dinner last week. The band
ate first at several small tables at the side of the
hall. On each table was a rope of green and blue
tinsel. A strange woman came up to me when I was alone
and took the tinsel from the table and put it on my head,
saying "it looks good on your white hair." I kept it on
all the evening. A couple came up to me and said they had
been watching me and thought I looked like their old
aunt in Arizona. Then the woman left and the man regaled
me with a resume' of his childhood and said he did not
know how much longer he had to live and was taking it one
day at a time. He told me about the several operations
he has had. Afterwards a young blond chick with a
camera came up and said "you look happy. May I take your
picture?" I humored her. Then last Wednesday there I
was in the weekly newspaper. So I am sending a copy.
You may laugh as much as you like. YOU never had your
picture in the paper when you were wearing a halo of
tinsel!!! I have had several copies saved for me by the
bunch here. I had that tinsel on all the time and did
not take it off until I went to bed and felt it on my
hair. Hunh!!

Hada's sister from Iowa has been here for several days.
She is to go home tomorrow and Hada is going to have a
little "tea" at the tiki this afternoon.

I am concerned about your finger. Keep after it and have
the proper thing done to it.

                    Mother

Love

XXXXX
00000
While she was taking my picture they were drawing
numbers for prizes. I won one -- it was a mug -- the kind
you drink from.

Dec. 15, 1981, age 94 (photo by Flossie Marsh
of the Tavernier, Fla., *Keynoter*).

a patient's case history from one young doctor when the doctor stopped talking. Mother said, "What was the diagnosis, Doctor?" Without looking up, he said, "Cryptorchidism." Mother wrote it down.

"Do you know what that is, Mary?" the doctor said with a tiny smirk.

"Yes. He had undescended testicles," she said quietly.

"Mary, you're a wonder!" said the delighted doctor.

MCML's father was a great reader, and he would read the whole newspaper after everyone had gone to bed. He sat at the big dining room table under the kerosene lamp and drummed his fingers on the wood incessantly. His wife would say finally, "Ike, will you stop that drumming and come to bed!"

After high school graduation in 1904, MCML traveled daily by train to Boston to the commercial school. There was a discussion in class about then-President Theodore Roosevelt. MCML took exception to the teacher's pronunciation of his name. "All right, Miss Mason. Why don't you write to him and find out the right way?"

And she did. Back came an engraved envelope with THE WHITE HOUSE on it. A folded sheet inside carried "Dear Miss Mason, The President thanks you for your interest and wants you to know that he prefers (or words to that effect)

Theodore Roosevelt."

written in a bold, readable hand. I think it was dated 1904 or 1905. I, Martha, looked in the dictionary and found:

1. Ro' ze velt; 2. spelling pron. roo' ze velt

MCML's great-great-granddaughter, Brianna Mason Perl, is the next one in the family with Mason in her name, so I have given her this letter. I figure it is worth now around $400. When Brianna is ready for college it may get her through September 2005.

At Mason's Rocks, Marblehead, Mass., Thursday, Aug. 8, 1912: (Back row) Frederic Brigham Litchman, Jonathan Breed Mason, Martha Betsy Mason, Henry Clarence Sparhawk Mason, Ernest Cole Mason, Annie Green Mason, Harold Kilgore Lord; (middle row) Coralie Mason Litchman, Isaac Wyman Mason, Jr., holding Elizabeth Ellen Lord, Elizabeth Ellen Cole Mason, Mary Cole Mason Lord, Helen Mason; (front) Edith May Mason, Florence Mason, Warren Mason, Alice Mason.

MARTHA MASON LORD GETCHELL was born in Sanford, Maine, and spent nearly 40 years of her married life in Great Falls, Virginia. But Marblehead, Massachusetts, home to several generations of her mother's family, holds fond memories. She recalls summer vacations there, on the North Shore 17 miles above Boston, "where early boyfriends dwelled and I did cartwheels at Crocker Park, my Uncle Jot took me out lobstering at dawn, and the whole harbor shore from the lighthouse to the Fort was outlined with lighted red Roman candles on the Fourth."

Martha and Nelson Getchell now make their home in Seneca, South Carolina. Nearby is an 85-year-old farmhouse they have converted into a shop that deals in the antique furniture, art and memorabilia they have collected all their lives.

MCML is her first book.

MCML / *Mary Cole Mason Lord, 1887-1988*

Book coordinator and editor: Jackie Pels
Design and production: David R. Johnson
Original transcription by Deborah Lord Boelter
Technical assistance: Werner Pels and Sharon Hatami

Lord family photos, except as noted. The postcard views of old Marblehead are from the collection of Martha and Nelson Getchell. Reproduced throughout the book are stitchery details from a quilt embroidered in 1903 by MCML's grandmother, Sallie Ashton High Cole Lamprell, at age 77. The panel on p. 69 is a portrait of her daughter (MCML's aunt) Sarah Abigail Cole Wadden (S.A.W.).

About the back cover photo: Mary Cole Mason, just out of high school herself in 1906, taught at Springvale Lincoln High School in Maine, coached and played on the girls' basketball team—and met her future husband, Harold Lord, who was a senior that year.

Composition by Archetype Typography, Berkeley, California
Printed and bound at Inkworks, Berkeley, California
Alkaline pH recycled paper (Revue by Monadnock)

Hardscratch Press
2358 Banbury Place
Walnut Creek, CA 94598
510/935-3422